Mighty Warren & the Dinos

Wendy Perry

ISBN 979-8-89130-954-8 (paperback)
ISBN 979-8-89345-097-2 (hardcover)
ISBN 979-8-89130-955-5 (digital)

Copyright © 2024 by Wendy Perry

All rights reserved. No part of this publication may be reproduced, distributed, or transmitted in any form or by any means, including photocopying, recording, or other electronic or mechanical methods without the prior written permission of the publisher. For permission requests, solicit the publisher via the address below.

Christian Faith Publishing
832 Park Avenue
Meadville, PA 16335
www.christianfaithpublishing.com

Printed in the United States of America

To my Grandma who planted the seed, "You can be anything, just be,"–I am.

To my Grandpa who always kept a smile on my face and a story in his heart.

Eternally grateful for your love and influence on my life.

Mighty Warren is growing up so big and so fast,
    That's amazing!
        Daily carving out his own personality.
            With a love of books, dinosaurs, wrestling with Dad
                Snuggles with Mom, full of wiggles for all...

"Shhhh! What do I hear? Can it be the sound of a dinosaurs' ROAR?"

A trillion tons of sheer strength and power,
    Pounding the ground, each step as if a magnificent earthquake
        occurred
Each step bringing destruction and fright,
    Surrounding the living room and couch
        T. Rex has been found!

The force of his tail swinging left,
    Swinging right with a fiery ROAR echoing across the land.
The stomp of his feet, gnashing of his teeth
    Destroying everything in reach. His strength unleashed.
His might to be envied and feared,
    "Oh no! What's next?

Mighty Warren has the agility of a fierce warrior.
    The maneuvers of a skilled craftsman
        An artist in his element-seek and destroy!
Yes, this little boy knows destruction and power all rolled up into one!

He swings his weapons of mass destruction,
> With sure feet and swift speed, he runs fast, hops over this and hops over that.

Only Mighty Warren can save his land!
> With his cape of strength and weapons nearby.

Mighty Warren so advanced and so strong.
Intimidated by none, feared by all.

Mighty Warren unleashes his arsenal of tricks, stones, mortar, and bones.

Defeating one for all. The fierce and mighty warrior,
Warren stands tall and strong!
Capturing the enemy, saving all!

Where is Mighty Warren?

He's riding so fast on his dino-mobile, surveying the destruction, only he can understand!

"Wow! Look at this! Look at that!" Mass destruction across our land!

A battle we had. The war is won! Until next time...

Riding his Dino-mobile, "Catch me if you can!".

Mighty Warren comes back to his surroundings.

It's Dad behind him, not a Dino.

"It's bedtime, Warren!"

Dad is gaining. Mighty Warren is Zooming—

Avoiding bedtime as fast as he can! The wind flying through his hair!

The noise of pistons firing!

Dirt and rock spewing! Zoom!

There he goes! His little legs peddling so fast. Defying the speed of light.

Dad is nearing. Mighty Warren thinks, *I gotta Zoom faster!*

He's gaining on me!

"Warren, it's bedtime!"

Then with one, quick sweep of Dad's big, strong hands, Mighty Warren is off to bed. He's off to dream about dinosaurs and their ROAR!

His books, snacks, and stuffed animals are patiently waiting for him!

Another productive day for a Mighty Warrior.

Another successful hunt and so much more...
Mighty Warren so big and so strong,
No match for dinos at all!
Good night, Mighty Warren!

About the Author

I was raised by my grandparents in California, both of whom were dramatic storytellers and writers. I was captivated by their knowledge and imagination. When I was nine and a half years old, I wrote my autobiography. I was so disappointed to have written only two paragraphs which was my whole, entire life. My grandmother said, "Wendy, you have to live life to write about it." I took those words to heart, and once my sons started building and living their lives, I began to live mine.

As I returned to writing poetry, my greatest muse has been my grandson, Warren. His big personality with a hint of mischief and a load of energy and animation has brought love and life to our family, and the birth of *Mighty Warren and the Dinos*.

Currently, I am living in New York. I love reading, running, music, playing my guitar, traveling, and writing poetry–I'm living my best life!

Printed in the USA
CPSIA information can be obtained
at www.ICGtesting.com
LVHW070719221024
794501LV00014B/204